Your Guide to Pho

Discover Delicious Pho Recipes - That You Can Make at Home!

BY: Valeria Ray

License Notes

Copyright © 2020 Valeria Ray All Rights Reserved

All rights to the content of this book are reserved by the Author without exception unless permission is given stating otherwise.

The Author have no claims as to the authenticity of the content and the Reader bears all responsibility and risk when following the content. The Author is not liable for any reparations, damages, accidents, injuries or other incidents occurring from the Reader following all or part of this publication.

Table of Contents

Introduction 6

1. Pho and beef noodle soup 7

2. Pho noodle soup with seafood 11

3. Gia lai—style double-bowl pho 16

4. Pho noodle soup with beef stew in red wine 21

5. Pho and chicken noodle soup 26

6. Stir-Fried Pho with Seafood 30

7. Glass Noodle Soup with Eel 34

8. Pho Omelet 39

9. Chicken Curry Pho 41

10. Crispy Pho with Choy Sum and Beef Stir-Fry 45

11. Fresh Pho Rolls 48

12. Vegan Pho Salad with Mushrooms 51

13. Pho noodle soup with beef stew 54

14. Pho Salad with Char Siu 57

15. Pho Salad with Beef and Tamarind Sauce 60

16. Glass Noodle Soup with Chicken 63

17. Pho noodle soup with roasted duck 67

18. Quang-Style Pho with Pork and Shrimp 72

19. Phnom Penh Noodle Soup 76

20. Pho Pizza 80

21. Shrimp and Noodle Pho 84

22. Roast pork noodle soup 86

23. Thai Shrimp Noodle Soup 89

24. Penang laksa 91

25. Egg flower noodle soup 93

BONUS: Appetizers 96

26. Spring rolls 97

27. San choy bau with cellophane noodles 101

28. Cubed Radish Kimchi 104

29. Mushrooms in Soy Sauce (Pyogo Bohsot) 106

30. Wontons 108

Conclusion 110

About the Author 111

Author's Afterthoughts 112

Introduction

Have you ever wanted to try pho at home but haven't a clue where or how to begin? If so, this recipe book is for you! In this recipe book, there are 30 aromatic, flavorful pho recipes that you'll be able to choose from. From Pho soup to Pho salad and Pho appetizers, there's plenty of options!

All the recipes in here are easy and straightforward and can be made by even the most beginner cook. So, choose a recipe and let's get started!

1. Pho and beef noodle soup

While traditional phở bò takes at least 8 hours to cook, this is a much easier version!

Time: 2 - 8 hours

Makes: 8 - 10 servings

Ingredients:

Broth

- 5 lb. beef bones
- 1 inch piece rock sugar, + more to taste
- 1 lb. beef brisket or flank, kept whole
- 1 tbsp salt, + more to taste
- Chicken stock powder, to taste
- 20 cups water
- 1 med yellow onion, peeled

Pho aroma

- Med yellow onion, nicely unpeeled and halved
- Thumb-size ginger knobs, cut lengthwise into 1/8-inch-thick slices
- 3 star anise
- 3 sprigs asian basil
- 1 tsp coriander seeds (optional)
- 1 tsp cloves (optional)
- 2 or 3 black cardamom pods
- 2 cinnamon sticks

Pho bowl

- 3 1/3 lb. cooked or fresh pho noodles
- 10½ oz beef, thinly sliced
- 1 yellow onion, sliced thinly, soaked in ice water for 16 mins, drained
- 3-5 scallions (green parts chopped; white bits whole, smashed, blanched)

Instructions:

For Broth: put the beef bones in a pot filled with water that covers them. Then, bring to boil cook for 5-10 mins, until all the impurities rise to the top. Drain the pot rinse your bones well under running water to wash away.

Next, place the bones in a pot with the beef brisket the water. Add the onion, 1 tbsp. salt, and thumb-size piece rock sugar to the pot. Bring to boil, lower heat to low, simmer, uncovered. From time to time, skim off the scum.

For Pho aroma: heat the onion 1/2s ginger slices directly on top of an open flame on the stove until a bit charred on all sides. Peel the onion carefully. Rinse the onion ginger under warm water remove off the charred.

Toast the cinnamon sticks, star anise, black cardamom pods, cloves (if using), coriander seeds (if using) in a pan on med-low heat until fragrant, about 2 mins. Place these spices in a spice ball/large tea/spice bag(s) or just wrap in a piece of cheesecloth. Add in the spices the charred onion ginger into the stockpot 30-45 mins before serving.

When you pierce the meat see no pink water coming out, it is cooked. Then, remove soak in a large bowl of cold water for 5 mins. Drain, then thinly slice into bite-size pieces. Put aside.

Next, remove the onion halves from your pot, which will make the Broth less clear. Then, continue to simmer for at least a few more hours on low heat. The Broth should simmer at least 2 hrs. approximately from the beginning of making the recipe and up to 8 hrs.

Season with salt, sugar, stock powder.

To assemble the bowls: top each bowl 1/3 full of noodles. Top with beef, the onion slices, chopped scallions, blanched scallions.

Then, ladle the hot Broth over the noodles.

Lastly, serve with a platter of the herbs, lime wedges bean sprouts, along with the sriracha hoisin sauce.

2. Pho noodle soup with seafood

Feel free to use other kinds of seafood in this soup (phở hải sản), such as mussels, scallops, salmon, or abalone.

Time: 2 to 8 hours

Makes: 8 to 10 servings

Ingredients:

Broth

- 6 lb. beef bones
- 20 cups water
- 1 med yellow onion, peeled
- 1 tbsp salt
- 2 thumb-size pieces rock sugar, + more to taste
- 1 onion, peeled
- Chicken stock powder, to taste

Seafood

- 7 oz (200 g) whole shrimp
- 7 oz (200 g) cuttlefish, with skin, quill, eyes, interiors, and ink sacs removed
- 14 oz (400 g) shell-on clams or mussels, put in salted water to keep fresh
- 3½ oz (100 g) fish balls

Pho aroma

- 3 shallots
- 4 slices ginger (cut long into 1/8 inch slices)
- 1 cinnamon stick
- 2 Black cardamom pods

Pho bowl

- 3 sprigs asian basil
- 3 sprigs sawtooth herb
- 3 1/3 lb. fresh/cooked pho noodles
- 1 onion, sliced very thin, put in ice water for 15 mins drained
- 3 sprigs asian basil
- 1 lime, cut into wedges
- 1 lb. bean sprouts, blanched

(optional)

- 3-5 scallions (green parts chopped; white parts whole, smashed, blanched)
- 3 bird's eye chili pepper, thinly sliced
- Sriracha (optional)

Instructions:

For Broth: place the beef bones in a large stockpot filled with enough water to cover it. Bring to boil cook for 5-10 mins, until the impurities come to the top. Drain the pot wash the bones under water.

Put the bones in a pot with the water. Add the onion, 1 tbsp. salt, and 2 thumb-size pieces rock sugar to the stockpot. Bring to boil, lower heat simmer, uncovered, for 2 to 8 hours—the longer the better. From time, skim off the scum. After 1 hour, remove the onion. Season the **Broth** to taste with salt, rock sugar, and chicken stock powder.

To prepare the seafood: in a large pan, toast the shrimp (without oil) over high heat until they turn completely orange. Remove from the heat and let cool. Peel and devein. Reserve the shrimp shells for later use.

Slice the cuttlefish in half along the spine. On each half, with the tip of a very sharp knife, score parallel diagonal lines from end to end, about halfway into the flesh. Don't cut all the way through. Do again in the other direction to make a crisscross pattern. Then cut into 2-inch (5 cm) squares.

For Pho aroma: heat the shallots and ginger slices directly on top of a flame till slightly charred on all of the sides. Peel then rinse the shallots and ginger under warm water and remove off the charred.

Toast the cinnamon stick and cardamom pods in a pan over med low heat for 1 to 2 minutes, or until fragrant.

Place all of the Pho aroma ingredients and the reserved shrimp shells in a spice ball/large tea/spice bag(s), or wrap securely in a piece of cheesecloth. Add to the pot 30-45 minutes before serving.

Extract the Broth into a separate pot. Bring to a boil.

Add the clams to this pot and cook until they open. Remove with a slotted spoon move to a plate.

Add the cuttlefish cook for 2 mins, or until it curls up and turns opaque. Remove with a slotted spoon move to a plate. Repeat with the fish balls.

To assemble the bowls: fill each bowl 1/3rd full of noodles (about a handful of noodles). Arrange the clams, cuttlefish, shrimp, and fish balls on top of the noodles. Top with onion slices, blanched and chopped scallions. Put the hot **Broth** over the noodles to fill the bowls.

Serve with the herbs, bean sprouts (if using), lime, chili pepper slices, along with the hoisin sauce sriracha.

3. Gia lai–style double-bowl pho

This dish is a great noodle variation that combines pork and beef. It is unique to gia lai, a highland city in central vietnam.

Time: 1 hour 30 minutes

Makes: 6 servings

Ingredients:

Broth

- 2 lb. (907 g) beef, pork, or chicken bones
- 12 cups (3 qt, or 3 l) water
- 1 med yellow onion, peeled
- 2 thumb-size pieces rock sugar
- 2 tsp salt, plus more to taste
- 6-inch (15 cm) pieces daikon, peeled and sliced into six 1-inch-thick
- (2.5 cm) rounds chicken stock powder, to taste

Toppings

- 7 oz (200 g) ground pork salt, to taste
- Black pepper, to taste
- 2 oz (56 g) pork fatback,
- finely diced
- 3 tbsp (30 g) garlic, minced
- ½ tsp sugar
- 3 shallots, thinly sliced
- 12 beef balls, thawed

Pho bowl

- 14 oz (400 g) dried gia lai–style noodles (bánh phở khô gia lai) or hủ tiếu dai noodles, soaked in room temperature water for 15 minutes and drained
- 3 cups (300 g) bean sprouts
- 2 tbsp (32 g) hoisin sauce, plus more for dipping
- 2 tbsp (30 ml) soy sauce
- 7 oz (200 g) beef sirloin or eye of round, very thinly sliced 5 scallions, chopped
- 3 sprigs cilantro, chopped
- 1 head soft-leaf lettuce
- 3 sprigs Asian basil
- 2 bird's eye chili peppers, thinly sliced
- 1 lime, cut into wedges
- Sriracha, for dipping

Instructions:

For **Broth**: place the bones in a large stockpot filled with enough water to cover them. Bring to a boil and cook the bones for 5-10 mins, until the impurities come to the top. Drain rinse the bones well under water.

Place the bones in a large stockpot with the water. Add the onion, rock sugar, 2 tsp salt, and daikon rounds. Bring to boil, then lower to low, simmer, uncovered, for 1 to 2 hours. Occasionally skim off the scum.

For toppings: in a med bowl, season the ground pork with salt and pepper. Add a bit of water to the bowl and stir to separate the meat chunks.

Add the diced fat back to a med pan over med-high heat. Cook and stir to render the fat, about 5 minutes. When the fat pieces shrink and turn golden brown, remove them with a slotted spoon and transfer them (pork rinds) to a bowl. Set aside.

Add the garlic to the pork fat left in the pan and cook and stir over med-low heat until golden brown. Remove the fried garlic from the pan with a slotted spoon, transfer to a bowl, and mix with the sugar, which helps keep the garlic crispy. Set aside.

Add the shallots to the pork fat left in the pan and cook and stir over med-low heat until golden brown, about 1 minute. Remove the fried shallot with a slotted spoon and transfer to a bowl. Set aside.

Add the ground pork to the remaining fat in the pan and stir-fry over med heat until it is cooked through. Use your spatula to break up any chunks. Turn off the heat.

Make a cross incision halfway through the beef balls, then add them to the **Broth** (close to serving time) and cook for 5 minutes. Remove with a slotted spoon and transfer to an ice-water bath—this is to prevent discoloring and maintain a springy texture.

Season with salt chicken stock powder.

To assemble the Pho bowls: add a handful of the gia lai–style noodles and some beansprouts to a noodle strainer. Put into a pot of boiling water for 30 seconds to blanch. Drain and toss with a tsp each of hoisin sauce and soy sauce until fully coated.

Repeat for remaining servings.

Fill each serving bowl 1/3rd full of noodles. For each bowl, using a ladle, submerge a few slices of beef into the simmering **Broth** to blanch for 5 seconds. Drain place on top of the noodles, along with 2 tbsp. ground pork, 2 beef balls, and a tsp each of fried garlic, fried shallot, and pork rinds.

Fill separate serving bowls one-half to two-thirds full of the hot **Broth** (maybe some bones, too), season with black pepper, and garnish with chopped scallions and cilantro.

Serve with the lettuce, chilli pepper slices, lime and Asian basil along with the hoisin sauce sriracha.

4. Pho noodle soup with beef stew in red wine

The red wine, bay leaves, and butter are what make this recipe more Western. Sautéing the onion in oil and adding the butter later helps maintain the butter smell and flavor.

Time: 1 hour

Makes: 5 servings

Ingredients:

Beef

- 1 lb. (454 g) beef flank or brisket, cut into 1 x 2-inch (2.5 x 5 cm) cubes
- 1 tbsp (10 g) garlic, minced or grated
- 1 tbsp (6 g) ginger, minced or grated
- ½ tsp five-spice powder
- 1 tsp sugar
- 1 tsp salt
- 1 tsp chicken stock powder
- ½ tsp black pepper
- ½ cup (120 ml) red wine, divided

Pho aroma

- 2 shallots or 1 small yellow onion
- 1 thumb-size ginger knob, cut into 1/8-inch-thick (3 mm) slices
- 2 coriander roots
- 1 cinnamon stick
- 1 star anise
- 1 black cardamom pod

Broth

- 8 cups (2 qt, or 2 L) beef Broth
- 2 tbsp (30 ml) vegetable oil
- ½ med yellow onion, diced
- 1 tbsp (16 g) tomato paste
- 1 tbsp (15 g) unsalted butter
- 2 bay leaves salt, to taste
- Rock sugar, to taste
- 3 tbsp (22 g) cornstarch
- ½ cup (120 ml) water

Pho bowl

- 2 lb. (907 g) fresh/cooked pho noodles
- 3 sprigs Asian basil, chopped
- 3 sprigs sawtooth herb, chopped
- 2 bird's eye chili peppers, thinly sliced
- 1 lime, cut into wedges
- Salt-Pepper-Lime sauce

Instructions:

For beef: In a large bowl, combine the beef cubes with the garlic, ginger, five-spice powder, sugar, salt, stock powder, black pepper, and ¼ cup (60 ml) of the red wine. Let be in the refrigerator for 2 hrs.

For Pho aroma: Heat the shallots, ginger slices, and coriander roots directly on top of a flame until a bit charred on all sides. Peel, then rinse the shallots, ginger, coriander under warm water remove off the charred bits.

Toast the cinnamon stick, star anise, and cardamom pod in a pan over med-low heat for 1 to 2 minutes, or until fragrant.

Place all of the Pho aroma ingredients in a spice ball or large tea or spice bag(s), or wrap securely in a piece of cheesecloth.

For Broth: Add the beef Broth to a large stockpot and bring to a boil. Drop the spice bag into the pot, reduce the heat to low, and simmer, uncovered, for 30 minutes to infuse the Broth with the pho aroma.

Heat the vegetable oil in a pressure cooker over med-high heat. Add the onion, then cook stir until translucent. Add the marinated beef cubes and cook and stir until no longer pink on the outside.

Add the tomato paste, butter, bay leaves, and remaining ¼ cup (60 ml) red wine to the pressure cooker. Pour in enough Broth to cover the beef, about 1 cup (235 ml). Cover and cook for 15 minutes over low heat. Turn off the pressure cooker and let it cool down.

Remove the spice bag from the stockpot, then transfer the Broth to the pressure cooker. Cover and bring to a boil.

Season with salt and rock sugar. (I use unsalted beef Broth, so I add 1½ tsp salt and 2 tsp rock sugar.)

Dilute the cornstarch in the water, then pour into the pressure cooker to slightly thicken the Broth.

To assemble the bowls: Fill each bowl 1/3rd full of noodles. Ladle the beef stew over the noodles. Garnish with Asian basil and sawtooth herb. Serve with chili pepper slices, lime wedges, and Salt-Pepper-Lime Sauce for dipping the beef.

5. Pho and chicken noodle soup

Delicious pho noodle soup with chicken.

Time: 2 - 8 hours

Makes: 8 - 10 servings

Ingredients:

Broth

- 5 lb. chicken bones
- 1 inch piece rock sugar, + more to taste
- 1 lb. chicken breasts
- 1 tbsp salt, + more to taste
- 20 cups water
- 1 med yellow onion, peeled
- Chicken stock powder, to taste

Pho aroma

- Med yellow onion, unpeeled and halved
- Thumb-size ginger knobs, cut lengthwise into 1/8-inch-thick slices
- 3 star anise
- 2 cinnamon sticks
- 2 or 3 black cardamom pods
- 3 sprigs Asian basil
- 1 tsp cloves (optional)
- 1 tsp coriander seeds (optional)

Pho bowl

- 3 1/3 lb. fresh or cooked pho noodles
- 10½ oz cooked chicken, thinly sliced
- 1 yellow onion, sliced thinly, soaked in ice water for 16 mins, drained
- 3-5 scallions (green parts chopped; white bits whole, smashed, blanched)

Instructions:

For Broth: put the bones in a pot filled with water that covers them. Bring to a boil cook for 5-10 mins, until all the impurities rise to the top. Drain the pot rinse the bones well under running water to wash away.

Place the bones in a pot with the chicken breasts the water. Add the onion, 1 tbsp. salt, and thumb-size piece rock sugar to the pot. Bring to boil, lower heat to low, simmer, uncovered. From time to time, skim off the scum.

For Pho aroma: heat the onion 1/2s ginger slices directly on top of an open flame on the stove until a bit charred on all sides. Peel the onion carefully. Rinse the onion ginger under warm water remove off the charred.

Toast the cinnamon sticks, star anise, black cardamom pods, cloves (if using), coriander seeds (if using) in a pan on med-low heat until fragrant, about 2 mins. Place these spices in a spice ball/large tea/spice bag(s) or just wrap in a piece of cheesecloth. Add in the spices the charred onion ginger into the stockpot 30-45 mins before serving.

When you pierce the meat see no pink water coming out, it is cooked. Remove soak in a large bowl of cold water for 5 mins. Drain and thinly slice into bite-size pieces. Put aside.

Remove the onion halves from the pot, which will make the Broth less clear. Continue to simmer for at least a few more hours on low heat. The Broth should simmer at least 2 hrs. from the beginning of making the recipe and up to 8 hrs.

Season with salt, sugar, stock powder.

To assemble the bowls: top each bowl 1/3rd full of noodles. Top with chicken, the onion slices, chopped scallions, blanched scallions.

Ladle the hot Broth over the noodles.

Serve with a platter of the herbs, bean sprouts, lime wedges, along with the hoisin sauce sriracha.

6. Stir-Fried Pho with Seafood

For this recipe (phở xào hải sản), use vegetables you prefer. Picking vegetables of various colors makes a pretty dish.

Time: 25 minutes

Makes 2 servings

Ingredients:

- Seafood Stir-Fry
- 3 ½ oz (100 g) cuttlefish, with skin, quill, eyes, interiors, and ink sacs removed
- 3½ oz (100 g) shrimp, peeled and deveined
- 1 tsp salt, plus more to taste
- Black pepper, to taste
- 1 tbsp (6 g) scallion, white part only, divided, minced
- 1 tbsp (10 g) garlic, divided, minced
- 1 tbsp (6 g) ginger, divided, minced
- 1 tsp cooking wine
- 1 tsp cornstarch
- 7 tbsp (105 ml) vegetable oil, divided
- ½ large carrot, thinly sliced
- 3½ oz (100 g) snow peas, strings removed
- 3½ oz (100 g) baby corn
- 7 oz (200 g) baby bok choy, rinsed and quartered
- 7 oz (200 g) dried pho noodles, soaked in water for 30 minutes and drained
- 3½ oz (100 g) fish cake, thinly sliced into bite-size pieces
- 2 oz (56 g) mushrooms (such as shiitake or straw)

Sauce

- 1 tbsp (18 g) oyster sauce
- 1 tsp sesame oil
- 2 tbsp (30 ml) soy sauce
- 2 tbsp (30 g) tomato sauce
- ½ cup (120 ml) water
- Garnish and Seasonings
- 3 sprigs cilantro, chopped
- ½ tsp white pepper
- Few drops sesame oil

Instructions:

For seafood stir-fry: Slice the cuttlefish in half along the spine. On each half, with the tip of a very sharp knife, score parallel diagonal lines from end to end, about halfway into the flesh and be careful not to cut all the way through. Repeat then in the opposite direction to create a crisscross pattern. Cut the fish into 2-inch (5 cm) squares.

In separate bowls, soak the cuttlefish and shrimp in salted water for 5 minutes, then drain.

In separate bowls, season the cuttlefish and shrimp with salt and black pepper, along with 1 tsp each of the scallion, garlic, ginger, cooking wine, and cornstarch. Mix well and set aside.

Bring a med pan of water to boil. Add the 1 tsp salt and 1 tbsp of the vegetable oil. Blanch the carrots for 2 minutes, then remove; blanch the snow peas for 2 minutes, then remove; and blanch the baby corn for 2 minutes, then remove. For the bok choy, dip the stems in the boiling water first and hold for 30 seconds, then drop in the whole leaves and blanch for another 30 seconds.

Heat 2 tbsp. (30 ml) of the oil in a large wok/pan over med-high heat. Add the remaining scallion, garlic, and ginger, and cook and stir until fragrant, about 15 seconds.

Add the shrimp to the wok and sear both sides for 1 to 2 minutes. Transfer set aside.

Add 2 tbsp. (30 ml) of the vegetable oil and the cuttlefish to the wok. Cook and stir until the cuttlefish curls and turns opaque, about 2 minutes. Transfer to a plate set aside.

For sauce: Combine the oyster sauce, sesame oil, soy sauce, tomato sauce, and water in a med bowl.

Add the remaining 2 tbsp. (30 ml) vegetable oil to the same wok the seafood was cooked in. Add the blanched vegetables and the sauce and cook and stir for 2 minutes.

Add the soaked noodles to the wok fry for 3 minutes. Return the shrimp and cuttlefish to the wok, tossing well and cooking for another 1 to 2 minutes.

Transfer the stir-fry to a serving platter and top with cilantro, white pepper, and sesame oil.

7. Glass Noodle Soup with Eel

In restaurants in Vietnam that serve this dish (miến lươn), you can choose soft eel (lươn mềm) or crispy eel (lươn giòn). I combine both versions in this recipe, but feel free to cook just one of them.

Time: 1 hour 30 minutes

Makes: 6 servings

Ingredients:

Broth

- 2¼ lb. (1 kg) pork bones
- 12 cups (3 qt, or 3 L) water
- 1 tbsp rice vinegar
- 1 tbsp salt
- 1 tsp rock sugar
- 1 med yellow onion, peeled and halved
- 5 shallots (2 kept whole and 3 thinly sliced), divided
- 2 slices ginger (length cut into 1 / 8-inch-thick, slices)
- Fish sauce, to taste
- Chicken stock powder, to taste

Eel

- 4 cups (1 qt, or 1 L) water
- 1 tsp salt, divided
- 1 lb. (454 g) eel
- ½ tsp black pepper
- ½ tsp turmeric powder
- ½ tsp ginger, grated
- ½ cup (60 g) cornstarch
- Vegetable oil, for frying

Noodle Bowl

- 14 oz (400 g) glass noodles, soaked in warm water for 10 minutes and drained
- ½ cup (30 g) Vietnamese mint Black pepper, chopped, to taste
- 3 scallions (green parts chopped; white parts kept whole, nicely smashed, and blanched)
- Black pepper, to taste
- 3 bird's eye chili peppers, thinly sliced
- 2 limes, cut into wedges
- Fish sauce

Instructions:

For Broth: Place the pork bones in a large pot. Fill with water to cover them. Add the vinegar and bring to a boil. Bring to a boil cook for 5-10 mins, until all the impurities rise to the top. Drain the pot rinse the bones well under running water to wash away.

Place the bones in a large stockpot and fill with the water. Add the 1 tbsp. salt, rock sugar, and onion. Bring to a boil skim off the scum. Reduce the heat to med-low simmer, uncovered, for 1 to 2 hours. Occasionally skim off the scum.

Heat the 2 whole shallots and ginger slices directly on top of a flame until a bit charred on all sides. Peel, then rinse the shallots and ginger under warm water and remove off the charred bits. Place all these ingredients in a large tea or spice ball or spice bag(s), or wrap securely in a piece of cheesecloth, then add to the stockpot during the last hour of cooking to enhance the aroma.

For eel: Add the water and ½ tsp of the salt to a small saucepan and bring to a boil. Add the eels and cook for 2 to 5 minutes depending on their size. When you see cracks on the eels' backs, they are cooked. Remove from the saucepan and let cool. Reserve the water in the saucepan.

Hold the heads of the eels with one hand, and use the thumb, index, and middle finger of your other hand to remove the flesh off the bone. If using large eels, you can fillet the flesh with a knife.

Bring the reserved water in the saucepan to a boil. Crush the eel bones in a mortar and pestle, add to the reserved water in the saucepan, and boil for another 15 minutes to release the sweetness. Strain to extract the eel **Broth**. Set aside.

Gather the eel flesh in a med bowl and combine with the remaining ½ tsp salt, black pepper, turmeric powder, and ginger. Divide into 2 parts, setting one part aside.

Spread the cornstarch on a plate and coat the sliced shallots and the other part of the seasoned eel in the cornstarch.

Place a small pan over med heat. Fill with oil to 2 inches (5 cm). Heat till the oil reaches 360°F. Fry the sliced shallots over med heat until golden brown. Remove transfer to a small bowl. Set aside.

In the same pan, fry the eel over med heat until golden brown, about 2 minutes. Remove put on a plate with paper towels to drain the excess oil.

Transfer the pork Broth to another stockpot and pour in the eel Broth. Next, season to taste with chicken stock powder and fish sauce. Bring the Broth to a boil.

To assemble the noodle bowls: For each bowl, place a handful of soaked glass noodles into your noodle strainer. Submerge then into the boiling **Broth** to blanch. Next, transfer the noodles to serving bowls. Top with some soft eel and crispy fried eel, Vietnamese mint, chopped scallions, blanched scallions, and black pepper. Ladle the hot soup over the eel and noodles, then top with fried shallots and chili pepper slices.

Serve with the lime wedges and fish sauce for dipping.

8. Pho Omelet

This omelet has the flavor of one of my favorite snacks from southern China: fried rice flour cakes with eggs (bột chiên).

Time: 10 minutes

Makes: 1 serving

Ingredients:

- 1 egg
- 1 tsp fish sauce
- ¼ tsp black pepper
- 1 scallion, chopped
- Vegetable oil, for frying
- 5½ oz (150 g) fresh/cooked pho noodles, separated
- Sweet chili sauce/sriracha, to taste, for serving
- Pickled Carrots Daikon, to taste, for serving

Instructions:

Crack egg in a bowl, then add the fish sauce the black pepper.

Fill a 9-inch (22 cm) pan with just enough vegetable oil to cover the bottom and heat to 375°F (180°C). Keep the heat at med put the noodles in the pan. Fry until almost golden brown.

Add in the beaten egg cook until it sets. Add the scallion in.

Serve with a bit of hot sauce the Pickled Carrots and Daikon.

9. Chicken Curry Pho

Lemongrass, different types of potatoes, and coconut milk are what distinguish Vietnamese chicken curry (bún cà ri gà) from other types of curries. The natural sweetness of the coconut water makes the curry heartier, but you can substitute chicken **Broth** or plain water. Feel free to use boneless chicken; just remember to reduce the cooking time.

Time: 1 hour

Makes: 6 servings

Ingredients:

Curry

- 2¼ lb. (1 kg) bone-in chicken, cut into bite-size pieces
- 1 tsp salt, plus more to taste
- 1 tsp sugar
- 1 tsp chicken stock powder
- ½ tsp black pepper
- 1 tbsp curry powder
- 1 lb. (454 g) potatoes, peeled, cut into 1-inch (2.5 cm) cubes, soaked in slightly salted water, and drained
- 1 lb. (454 g) sweet potatoes, peeled, cut into 1-inch (2.5 cm) cubes, soaked in slightly salted water, and drained
- 1 lb. (454 g) taro, peeled, cut into 1-inch (2.5 cm) cubes, soaked in slightly salted water, and drained
- ¼ cup (60 ml) plus 1 tbsp vegetable oil, divided
- 1 tbsp (10 g) garlic, minced
- 1 tbsp (10 g) shallot, minced
- 1 tbsp (6 g) ginger, minced
- 2 stalks lemongrass, bruised
- 1 cup (235 ml) coconut milk
- 6 cups (1.5 L) coconut water

Vermicelli Bowl

- 2 lb. (907 g) fresh or cooked rice vermicelli noodles
- 3 sprigs Asian basil
- 1 cup (100 g) bean sprouts
- 2 bird's eye chili peppers, thinly sliced
- ¼ cup (36 g) peanuts, crushed and roasted

Instructions:

For curry: In a large bowl, combine the chicken with the 1 tsp salt, black pepper, sugar, 1 tsp chicken stock powder, and curry powder. Let marinate in the refrigerator for at least 30 minutes or overnight.

Remove any excess water from the cubed potatoes, sweet potatoes, and taro using a paper towel. Heat ¼ cup (60 ml) of the vegetable oil in a large pan over high heat. Add the potatoes, sweet potatoes, and taro to the pan and fry until the outsides are golden brown and crispy—this is to keep them in shape and prevent a mushy texture in the curry. Remove from the pan place on a rack or a paper towel–lined tray to drain excess oil.

Heat the remaining 1 tbsp. vegetable oil in a large wok/pan over med-high heat. Add the garlic, shallot, and ginger to the pan, and cook and stir until fragrant, about 1 minute.

Add the marinated chicken stir well. Cook over high heat to sear the chicken on all sides. Transfer to a stockpot.

Add the lemongrass, coconut milk, and coconut water to the stockpot. Bring to a boil skim off the scum. Add the fried potatoes, sweet potatoes, and taro. Season to taste with salt and chicken stock powder. Reduce the heat to med-low and simmer for 30 to 45 minutes, or until the potatoes and chicken are fork-tender.

To assemble the vermicelli bowls: Fill each serving bowl one-third full of noodles (about a handful of noodles). Ladle the chicken curry over the noodles. Garnish with a few Asian basil leaves, bean sprouts, chili pepper slices, and crushed roasted peanuts.

10. Crispy Pho with Choy Sum and Beef Stir-Fry

This dish is one of the newer creations of pho restaurants in Vietnam. Choy sum (rau cải ngọt) is a leafy green vegetable commonly used in Chinese stir-fries. You can substitute the choy sum with bok choy or spinach.

Time: 25 minutes

Makes: 2 servings

Ingredients:

- 7 oz (200 g) beef tenderloin, thinly sliced against the grain
- Salt, to taste
- Black pepper, to taste
- 3 tbsp (45 ml) vegetable oil, divided, plus more for frying
- 1 tbsp (10 g) garlic, divided, minced
- 1 tsp plus 1 tbsp (18 g) oyster sauce, divided
- 1 tsp stock powder (optional)
- 2 tsp tapioca starch or cornstarch, divided, plus 1 / 3 cup (40 g) to coat the noodles
- 7 oz (200 g) fresh or cooked pho noodles
- 1 / 3 cup (80 ml) water
- 7 oz (200 g) choy sum, cut into 2-inch (5 cm) lengths and rinsed
- 2 egg yolks, lightly beaten
- ½ med yellow onion, peeled and cut into wedges
- 1 tbsp soy sauce
- 2 tbsp (20 g) crispy fried shallot (hành phi; you can buy these at an Asian food store), for garnish
- 1 bird's eye chili pepper, thinly sliced, for garnish

Instructions:

In a bowl, mix the beef with salt, black pepper, 1 tbsp. of the vegetable oil, 1 tsp of the minced garlic, 1 tsp of the oyster sauce, stock powder (if using), and 1 tsp of the tapioca starch. Give it a good mix and let it marinate for 15 minutes.

For crispy pho noodles, in a tray, separate the noodles with your hands. Mix the noodles with the beaten egg yolks, then fluff to coat with 1 / 3 cup (40 g) of the tapioca starch. Shake off the excess starch.

Place an 8-inch (20 cm) pan over med heat. Fill with oil to 2 inches (5 cm). Heat until the oil reaches 360°F.

Add the pho noodles to the saucepan one handful at a time and deep-fry over med heat until golden and crispy. The noodles might stick to each other but you should still see the individual strings. Remove from the pan place on a paper towel–lined plate to drain the excess oil. Divide the noodles between two serving plates.

In a bowl, add the remaining 1 tsp tapioca starch and the remaining 1 tbsp. (18 g) oyster sauce with the water to form a slurry. Set aside.

Heat 1 tbsp. of the vegetable oil in a large wok or pan over high heat. Add in the remaining 2 tsp garlic cook and stir until fragrant. Add the choy sum and fry until wilted, 3 to 4 minutes. Add the onion fry for 1 min. Stir in the soy sauce, then pour the stir-fried greens on top of the crispy noodles.

With the heat on high, add in the remaining 1 tbsp. vegetable oil to the wok and stir-fry the beef until no longer pink on the outside.

Pour the oyster-sauce slurry over the beef in the wok. Simmer for 1 minute until thickened, then pour the beef and sauce over the stir-fried greens.

Serve immediately with a sprinkle of black pepper and garnished with the fried shallot and chili pepper slices.

11. Fresh Pho Rolls

Here's a creative way to serve pho in the form of fresh spring rolls (phở cuốn), which originated in Hanoi.

Time: 1 hour

Makes: 10 to 15 rolls

Ingredients:

Rice Noodle Batter

- 1 cup (158 g) rice flour
- 1 cup (120 g) tapioca starch or cornstarch
- 2 cups (475 ml) water
- ½ tsp salt
- 2 tsp vegetable oil

Beef Stir-Fry

- 12 ½ oz (354 g) beef (such as rump steak), thinly sliced against the grain
- 2 tsp garlic, divided, minced
- 1 tsp ginger, minced
- ½ tsp salt
- 1 tsp chicken stock powder (optional)
- ½ tsp black pepper
- 1 tbsp vegetable oil, plus more for stir-frying
- 1 med yellow onion, thinly sliced lengthwise (optional)
- Fresh greens and herbs such as lettuce, mint, perilla, and cilantro

Instructions:

For rice noodle batter: Combine the rice flour, tapioca starch, water, salt, and vegetable oil in a large bowl. Let rest for 1 hour.

For beef stir-fry: Season the beef with 1 tsp of the garlic, ginger, salt, chicken stock powder (if using), black pepper, and 1 tbsp. vegetable oil. Mix well and let sit for 15 minutes.

Heat some oil in a wok/pan over high heat. Add the remaining 1 tsp garlic and cook and stir until fragrant. Add the beef fry over high heat until no longer pink on the outside. Do not overcook. Add the onion (if using) cook until slightly translucent, about 1 minute. Remove from the heat and set aside.

Place an 8-inch (20 cm) round or a 4 x 8-inch (10 x 20 cm) rectangular plate on the steaming rack in a steamer. Steam the plate for 1 to 2 minutes, until hot. Stir up the rice noodle batter add enough batter that will cover bottom of plate. Steam for 4-5 mins, until set and a bit translucent.

Use a spatula around the edges of the sheet carefully peel it off the plate. Repeat with the remaining batter. You can stack the rice sheets on top of each other when done.

To assemble the pho rolls: Place a rice sheet on a flat surface and top with some fresh greens, herbs, and beef. Lift the bottom end of the rice sheet and wrap it up over the filling, securing the roll closed gently but tightly.

Serve with some Fish Sauce Dressing.

12. Vegan Pho Salad with Mushrooms

Here's a simple, super-healthy recipe (phở trộn nấm), you can make in a jiffy. Using mushrooms, such as oyster, beech, enoki, shiitake, and straw mushrooms, or any other mushrooms that you prefer. It would be perfect to offer this dish in the fall after a mushroom harvest!

Time: 10 minutes

Makes: 4 servings

Ingredients:

- 3 tbsp (45 ml) vegetable oil, divided
- 2 shallots, thinly sliced
- 1 tbsp (10 g) garlic, divided, minced
- ¼ cup (61 g) tomato sauce
- ¼ cup (60 ml) soy sauce
- 2 tsp sugar
- ¼ tsp red chili flakes (optional)
- 1 2/3 lb. (750 g) fresh or cooked pho noodles
- 7 oz (200 g) various mushrooms, roots trimmed and separated (if using enoki) or sliced
- Salt, to taste Black pepper, to taste
- 2 scallions, finely chopped
- 2 tbsp (16 g) roasted sesame seeds
- 1 med tomato, sliced

Instructions:

Heat 2 tbsp. (30 ml) of the oil in a wok/pan over med heat. Add the shallots and fry until golden brown. Remove the shallots transfer to a small bowl. Set aside.

Add ½ tbsp. (5 g) of the minced garlic to the wok and cook and stir until fragrant.

Add the tomato sauce, soy sauce, sugar to the wok. Mix well and simmer for 30 seconds, until smooth. Add the chili flakes to the pan (if using). Turn off the heat. Transfer one-third of the sauce to a small bowl and set aside.

Separate the noodles with your fingers toss with the remaining sauce in the wok.

In a separate large pan, add the remaining 1 tbsp. vegetable oil and the remaining ½ tbsp. (5 g) garlic, and cook and stir until fragrant.

Add the mushrooms to the pan fry for 1-2 mins. Season with salt black pepper. Remove the pan from the heat.

Divide the noodles among the plates. Top with the mushrooms and then with chopped scallions, fried shallots roasted sesame seeds. Serve with the slices of the tomatoes reserved sauce for a dipping sauce.

13. Pho noodle soup with beef stew

In Vietnam, beef stew (bò kho) is commonly served as a hearty breakfast dish with freshly baked baguettes and a sunny-side-up egg. Some pho joints pour beef stew (sometimes diluted with beef Broth) over pho noodles, and voilà, you have a new member of the pho family: phở bò kho. Coconut water is the secret to a naturally sweet Broth.

Time: 1 hour 15 minutes

Makes: 6 to 8 servings

Ingredients:

- 3 lb. (1.4 kg) beef shank, tendon, and brisket (or shank or brisket),
- Cut into 1 x 2-inch (2.5 x 5 cm) cubes
- 2 tsp sugar, plus more to taste
- 1 tsp salt, plus more to taste
- 1 tsp chicken stock powder
- ½ tsp black pepper, plus more to taste
- 2 Tsp bò kho or five-spice powder
- 1 Tbsp (8 g) ginger, grated
- 2 Tbsp (30 ml) soy sauce
- 2 tbsp (20 g) garlic, divided, minced
- 1 tbsp vegetable oil
- 4 stalks lemongrass, cut into 3-inch (7.5 cm) lengths and bruised
- 3 star anise
- 1 cinnamon stick
- 1½ cups (368 g) tomato sauce or 3 tbsp (48 g) tomato paste
- 1 1/3 cups (315 ml) coconut water
- 6 cups (1.5 l) beef **Broth** or water
- 2 Lb. (907 g) carrots, peeled and cut into bite-size pieces
- 3 Tbsp (45 ml) annatto oil (page 170; optional)
- 2 Lb. (907 g) fresh or cooked pho noodles
- 3 Tbsp. (30 g) crispy fried shallot (hành phi; you can buy these at an Asian food store)
- 1 small yellow onion, sliced very thin, soaked in ice water for 15 minutes, and drained
- 3 sprigs sawtooth herb

- 3 sprigs Thai basil

Instructions:

In a bowl, mix the beef, 2 tsp sugar, 1 tsp salt, 1 tsp chicken stock powder, ½ tsp black pepper, bò kho, ginger, soy sauce, and 1 tbsp. (10 g) of the minced garlic. Mix well, cover, marinate in fridge for at least 1 hour or overnight.

Heat the oil in a large wok/pan over med-high heat. Add the remaining tbsp. (10 g) garlic, lemongrass, star anise, and cinnamon stick to the wok and cook and stir for 30 seconds to bring out the aroma. Add the marinated beef to the wok and stir-fry until no longer pink on the outside.

Add the tomato sauce, coconut water, and beef **Broth** to the wok. Bring to boil, cover, reduce the heat to low, and cook until the meat is tender, about 1-2 hrs. You can also use a pressure cooker, about 20 to 30 minutes.

When the beef is about tender, add in the carrots to the pan and cook until tender. Season with salt, sugar, chicken stock powder. Remove discard the star anise cinnamon stick. Add the annatto oil (if using).

Fill each serving bowl one-third full of noodles (about a handful of noodles). Ladle the beef stew over the noodles. Season with black pepper and garnish with fried shallot, onion slices, sawtooth herb, and Thai basil.

14. Pho Salad with Char Siu

This recipe (phở xíu) tastes simply divine, and the secret is roast red pork seasoning mix (char siu powder). Choose a pork shoulder that still has some fat on it, so the meat will be juicy.

Time: 40 minutes

Makes: 6 servings

Ingredients:

- 1.76 oz (50 g) roast red pork seasoning mix
- 2 tbsp (20 g) minced garlic
- 1 tbsp (6 g) grated ginger
- 1 tbsp salt
- 1 tbsp soy sauce
- 1 tbsp sesame oil
- 1 tbsp (18 g) oyster sauce
- 2 tbsp (40 g) honey
- 3 tbsp (45 ml) vegetable oil, divided
- 1 tbsp cooking wine
- 3 tbsp (45 ml) plus ½ cup (120 ml) water, divided
- 1 lb. (454 g) pork shoulder, cut into long bars, about 1 x 2 inches (2 x 4 cm) thick
- 2 lb. (907 g) fresh or cooked pho noodles
- 1 head leaf lettuce, torn into small pieces
- 2 cups (200 g) bean sprouts, blanched
- 3 sprigs Asian basil
- 3 bird's eye chili peppers, thinly sliced, for garnish
- ½ cup (80 g) crispy fried shallot (hành phi; you can buy these at an Asian food store), for garnish

Instructions:

Combine the roast red pork seasoning mix, garlic, ginger, salt, soy sauce, sesame oil, oyster sauce, honey, 1 tbsp. of the vegetable oil, wine, and 3 tbsp. (45 ml) of the water in a large bowl, and stir to dissolve. Add the pork to the bowl and submerge in the marinade. Cover with plastic wrap. Let marinate in fridge for at 2 hours or overnight.

Preheat the oven to 500°F (250°C). Place the marinated pork on a baking tray lined with aluminum foil, reserving the marinade. Broil for 15 minutes, then flip and cook for another 20 minutes at 400°F (200°C).

Remove from the oven let cool on a rack for 20 minutes, then cut into thin slices.

Heat the remaining 2 tbsp. (30 ml) oil in a wok/pan over med heat.

Add the reserved marinade to a small saucepan and dilute with the remaining ½ cup (120 ml) water to make a sauce. Bring to a boil. Remove from the heat.

To assemble the Pho bowl, fill each serving bowl one-third full of noodles (about a handful of noodles). Add 2 tbsp. (30 ml) of the sauce to each bowl and mix to coat the noodles.

Place some lettuce, blanched bean sprouts, and Asian basil around the sides of the bowls, and arrange 5 or 6 slices of Char siu on top.

Garnish with chili pepper slices and the fried shallot and mix well before serving.

15. Pho Salad with Beef and Tamarind Sauce

This quick and easy summer salad is one that you're sure to enjoy on those extremely hot days when you don't really feel like eating anything, let alone cooking.

Time: 10 minutes

Makes: 4 to 6 servings

Ingredients:

- 1 lb. (454 g) beef (such as rump steak), thinly sliced against the grain
- Salt, to taste
- Black pepper, to taste
- 2 tbsp (20 g) garlic, divided, minced
- 1 tbsp (10 g) shallot, divided, minced
- 1 tsp chicken stock powder
- 1 tbsp (18 g) oyster sauce
- 1 tbsp vegetable oil, plus more for stir-frying
- 1 tsp tapioca starch or cornstarch
- 5 oz (150 g) tamarind pulp 2 cups (475 ml) water
- 1 to 2 tbsp (15 to 30 g) butter
- ½ cup (100 g) sugar or palm sugar
- ½ cup (120 ml) fish sauce
- 2 lb. (907 g) fresh or cooked pho noodles, tossed with some vegetable oil
- 1 lb. (454 g) bean sprouts, blanched
- 3 sprigs Asian basil
- 3 sprigs Vietnamese balm
- 3 sprigs mint
- ¼ cup (36 g) roasted peanuts, crushed, for garnish
- 3 bird's eye chili peppers, thinly sliced, for garnish

Instructions:

In a bowl, mix the beef with salt, black pepper, 1 tbsp. (10 g) of the garlic, ½ tbsp. (5 g) of the shallot, chicken stock powder, oyster sauce, 1 tbsp. vegetable oil, and tapioca starch. Mix well, cover, then marinate in the fridge for 30 minutes.

Add the tamarind pulp and water to a small saucepan. Bring to boil cook for 5 to 10 minutes, until the pulp breaks up. Strain the pulp using a sieve to get the tamarind sauce. Set aside.

Add the butter to a med pan over med heat. Add the remaining 1 tbsp. (10 g) garlic and the remaining ½ tbsp. (5 g) shallot to the pan and cook and stir until fragrant. Add the tamarind sauce, sugar, and fish sauce to the pan. Taste adjust as needed to achieve a balance of flavor. Turn off the heat and let cool.

Heat some oil in a wok/pan over high heat. Add the beef and stir-fry until the beef is no longer pink on the outside, 3 to 4 minutes. Don't overcook.

To assemble the bowls, fill each bowl 1/3rd full of noodles and drizzle the sweet-and-sour tamarind sauce over the top. Give it a good mix, then add blanched bean sprouts and herbs. Top with the stir-fried beef and garnish with a sprinkle of crushed roasted peanuts and some chili pepper slices.

16. Glass Noodle Soup with Chicken

This soup (miến gà) is simple to cook and doesn't require too many herbs or sauces. It is a hearty noodle soup I like to prepare for breakfast on the weekend.

Time: 1 hour

Makes: 4 servings

Ingredients:

- 1 whole chicken (about 2½ lb., or 1.2 kg)
- 1 tbsp salt, plus more for the chicken and to taste
- 1 scallion
- 4 slices ginger (cut lengthwise into 1/8-in-thick, or 3 mm, slices), divided
- 2 small yellow onions, peeled and halved, divided
- 6 shallots (3 kept whole and 3 thinly sliced), divided
- 5 coriander roots
- 1 set chicken internal organs (liver, heart, gizzard), rinsed and thinly sliced (optional)
- ½ tsp fish sauce, plus more for serving (optional)
- ½ tsp black pepper, plus more to taste (optional)
- ½ tsp chicken stock powder (½ tsp is optional)
- 1 tsp shallot, minced (optional)
- 3 kaffir lime leaves, rolled and sliced into fine threads
- Sugar, to taste
- 1 tbsp vegetable oil
- 14 oz (400 g) glass noodles, soaked in warm water for 10 minutes and drained
- ½ cup (30 g) Vietnamese mint, chopped
- 1 lime, cut into wedges, for serving
- 3 bird's eye chili peppers, thinly sliced, for serving

Instructions:

Rub the chicken with salt. Optional: Rinse the chicken well under cold running water, inside and out. Insert the scallion and 2 slices of the ginger into its cavity.

Add the chicken to a stockpot. Fill with enough water to cover it. Add the 1 tbsp. salt and one of the onions. Bring to a boil, and then skim off the scum, if any. Reduce to low simmer, uncovered. From time, skim off the scum. Depending on the type of chicken, it may take from 15 minutes to an hour to cook.

Heat the remaining onion, remaining 2 ginger slices, 3 whole shallots, coriander roots directly on top of a flame till a bit charred on all sides. Peel the onion and shallots, then rinse the onion, shallots, ginger, and coriander under warm running water and scrape off the charred bits. Place all these ingredients in a spice ball or large tea or spice bag(s), or wrap securely in a piece of cheesecloth, then add to the stockpot to enhance the aroma.

If using internal organs, season with ½ tsp each of the fish sauce, black pepper, and chicken stock powder, along with the minced shallot. Set aside.

When you pierce the meat no pink water comes out, it is cooked. Remove the chicken from the pot and let cool. Shred the meat into thin strips. Lightly season the shredded chicken with salt, black pepper, and the lime leaf threads.

For a heartier Broth, return the chicken bones to the stockpot and cook for an additional 30 to 60 minutes. Season to taste with salt, sugar, chicken stock powder (if using).

Heat the vegetable oil in a large wok or pan over med heat. Add the sliced shallots fry till golden brown. Keep the heat on med and immediately remove the fried shallots with a slotted spoon and transfer to a small bowl. Set aside.

Add the internal organs (if using) to the oil in the pan and stir-fry over high heat until cooked, about 2 minutes.

To assemble the bowls, add a handful of the softened glass noodles to each serving bowl. Top with the shredded chicken, the shallots, and some mint. Put the hot soup over the chicken and noodles.

Serve.

17. Pho noodle soup with roasted duck

This recipe comes out best if you can roast the duck in an oven with an auto-rotation function.

Time: 2 hours 30 minutes

Makes: 8 to 10 servings

Ingredients:

Duck

- 2 thumb-size ginger knobs, peeled, divided
- 1 tsp salt
- 1 whole duck (about 3 1/3 lb., or 1.5 kg)
- 5 or 6 shallots, divided
- 1 tbsp five-spice powder
- 1 tbsp garlic powder
- 2 tbsp (36 g) oyster sauce
- 1 tsp cooking wine or rượu mai quế lộ (rose cooking wine) 1 tsp salt
- ½ tsp black pepper
- 2 tsp sugar
- 1 tsp chicken stock powder
- ½ tsp annatto powder or paprika

Broth

- 16 cups (4 qt, or 4 l) water
- 4-5 lb. chicken

Bones

- 1 med yellow onion, halved, divided
- 1 tbsp salt, plus more to taste
- 1 tsp rock sugar, plus more to taste
- 10 dried sea worms (sá sùng), cut into 3-inch (7.5 cm) lengths, or 3 or 4 dried squids (optional)
- 3 star anise
- 1 cinnamon stick
- Chicken stock powder, to taste

Duck glaze

- 2 tbsp (30 ml) rice vinegar
- 1 tbsp (20 g) maltose or honey
- ½ tsp annatto powder or paprika

Pho bowl

- 3 sprigs Asian basil
- 3 1/3 lb. (1.5 kg) fresh/cooked pho noodles
- 3-6 scallions (green bits chopped; white bits whole, smashed, and blanched)
- 1 lb. (454 g) bean sprouts, blanched
- 2 limes, cut into wedges
- 3 sprigs sawtooth herb
- 3 bird's eye chili peppers, thinly sliced

Instructions:

For duck: in a mortar and pestle, roughly crush 1 knob of ginger with the salt. Rub crushed ginger all over the duck, inside and out. Optional: rinse the duck well under cold water and drain.

For duck marinade, in a small bowl, combine the five-spice powder, garlic powder, oyster sauce, cooking wine, salt, black pepper, sugar, chicken stock powder, and annatto powder. Rub this mixture all around and inside the duck.

From the remaining ginger knob, cut 6 lengthwise slices, 1/8 inch (3 mm) thick. Insert 3 slices into the duck cavity, along with 2 or 3 peeled shallots. Set aside the remaining 3 ginger slices. Use a bamboo skewer to stitch and seal its cavity so that the ginger, shallots, and juices don't fall out while the duck is roasting. Let marinate in fridge for 3-5 hours.

For Broth: fill a large stockpot with the water and add the chicken bones, an onion half, 1 tbsp. salt, and 1 tsp rock sugar. Bring to boil, reduce to low, simmer, uncovered, for 1 to 2 hours. From time, remove the scum.

For duck glaze: combine the vinegar, maltose, and annatto powder, and brush all over the bird, starting with the first rotation and again at every rotation, for a shiny, crispy skin. Roast the duck in an oven that is heated to 400°f (200°c) for 1 hour, rotating every 20 mins.

In a pan over med heat (without oil), toss the dried sea worms (if using), until fragrant and slightly golden. The dried sea worms will release lots of sand. Cut the sea worm tube open and rinse well a few times to get rid of all the sand. Insert into a filter

Bag and place in the Broth 30 to 45 minutes before serving.

For Pho aroma: heat the remaining 3 shallots and remaining 3 slices ginger directly on top of a flame till a bit charred on all sides. Peel then rinse the shallots and ginger under warm water and remove off the charred bits.

Toast the cinnamon stick star anise in a pan over med-low heat for 1 to 2 minutes, or until fragrant.

Place all of the Pho aroma ingredients in a spice ball or large tea or spice bag(s), or wrap securely in a piece of cheesecloth. Add to the stockpot 30 to 45 minutes before serving, so the aroma stays fresh and tempting.

Cut the remaining onion half into paper-thin slices, soak in ice water for 15 minutes, and drain.

After 1 hour of roasting the duck, increase the oven temperature to 500°f (250°c) and broil for another 10 minutes, rotating once, so the duck skin is evenly golden. Remove from the oven and let rest until cool. Gather the running juices from the cooked duck into a bowl to serve as a dipping sauce later. Before serving, debone and slice the duck meat into 1/8-inch-thick (3 mm) slices.

Season the Broth to taste with salt, rock sugar, and/or chicken stock powder.

To assemble the bowls: fill each bowl 1/3rd full of noodles. Top with duck meat and ladle the hot soup into the bowls. Top with chopped scallions, blanched scallions, and onion slices.

Serve with a plate of the herbs, bean sprouts, lime , chili pepper slices, along with the reserved duck roast juices as a dipping sauce or to be added to the **Pho bowl** for more flavor.

18. Quang-Style Pho with Pork and Shrimp

This dish is the ultimate comfort food. This recipe with pork and shrimp is the most traditional one.

Time: 45 minutes

Makes: 10 servings

Ingredients:

- 1 lb. (454 g) pork belly, thinly sliced
- 1 tbsp (10 g) shallot, minced
- 1¼ tsp turmeric powder, divided (¼ tsp is optional)
- 1 tsp salt, divided, plus more to taste
- 1 tsp black pepper, divided
- 3 tbsp (45 ml) fish sauce, divided, plus more to taste
- 1 lb. (454 g) white shrimp, shell-on, with legs, heads, and tails trimmed
- 4 tbsp (60 ml) vegetable oil, divided
- 1 tbsp (10 g) garlic, minced
- 1 lb. (454 g) fresh tomatoes, peeled, seeds removed, and pureed, or canned pureed tomatoes
- 1 tbsp sugar
- 5 cups (1.2 L) chicken or pork **Broth** (you can also use water)
- Chicken stock powder, to taste (optional)
- 17½ oz (500 g) dried mì Quảng noodles
- 2 tbsp (30 ml) rice vinegar or fresh lime juice
- 1 trunk banana blossom
- 3½ oz (100 g) mint leaves, stems removed
- 3½ oz (100 g) perilla leaves, stems removed
- 1 large head leaf lettuce
- 10½ oz (300 g) bean sprouts
- 5 scallions, chopped
- 3½ oz (100 g) cilantro, chopped
- ½ cup (72 g) roasted peanuts, crushed
- 2 rice crackers broken into pieces

- 2 limes, cut into wedges, for serving
- 3 bird's eye chili peppers, thinly sliced, for serving

Instructions:

Add the pork, minced shallot, 1 tsp of the turmeric powder, ½ tsp each of the salt and black pepper, and 1 tbsp. of the fish sauce to a large bowl, and mix well. Season the shrimp with the remaining ½ tsp each salt and black pepper in a separate bowl and mix well. Set both bowls aside for 30 minutes.

Heat 1 tbsp. of the vegetable oil in a stockpot or a med saucepan over med heat. Add the minced garlic and cook and stir until fragrant.

Add 1 tbsp. of the fish sauce and the pureed tomatoes to the stockpot. Simmer over low heat for 5 mins, until slightly thickened.

Next, meanwhile, in a separate large pan, heat 1 tbsp. of the vegetable oil over high heat and cook and stir the pork for about 5 minutes. Transfer it to a clean bowl.

Add 1 tbsp. of the vegetable oil to the same pan the pork was cooked in and cook and stir the shrimp over high heat for 1 minute. Add the sugar and cook and stir for another minute. Add the remaining 1 tbsp. fish sauce and simmer, uncovered, over low heat, until the sauce is almost evaporated, 8 to 10 minutes

Next, when the tomato sauce thickens, add the chicken **Broth** to your pot. Bring to your boil. Then, add the sautéed pork belly. Adjust the **Broth** to your taste. (I add 2 tbsp., or 30 ml, fish sauce; 2 tsp chicken stock powder; and 1 tsp salt.) The **Broth** should be a bit saltier than a soup, but less salty than a sauce. Unlike pho noodle soup, we use a lot less **Broth** for each bowl of mì Quảng.

Cook the noodles following package instructions. Add the remaining 1 tbsp. vegetable oil to the boiling water. If you want to color the noodles yellow, add the remaining ¼ tsp turmeric powder 1 minute before the noodles are fully cooked.

To prepare the banana blossom, add the vinegar to a large bowl of cold water. Remove and discard the thick outer layers of the banana blossom and any flowers in between. Cut up into paper-thin rings. Put the rings immediately into the water to prevent discoloring. Rinse the rings twice under cold running water and drain.

Cut the mint and perilla leaves and the lettuce into thin strips, about 1 inch (2.5 cm) thick. Mix with the banana blossom bean sprouts.

To prepare, fill the serving bowls half-full of fresh herbs and lettuce, then place a handful of noodles on top of the greens. Top with a few shrimp and pork belly slices, and put the **Broth** over. Top with chopped scallion and cilantro, some crushed peanuts, and a piece of rice cracker.

Serve with the lime wedges, chili pepper slices, and a plate of the remaining fresh greens. Mix well with chopsticks before serving.

19. Phnom Penh Noodle Soup

This popular noodle dish (hủ tiếu) from Saigon is a delicious and easy soup!

Time: 1 hours 30 minutes

Makes: 8 servings

Ingredients:

Broth

- 1 dried squid (hand size)
- ½ cup (90 g) dried shrimp
- 3 1/3 lb. pork bones
- 20 cups water
- 1 med yellow onion, peeled
- 2 thumb-size pieces rock sugar
- 1 tbsp salt 6-inch (15 cm) piece daikon, peeled and cut into six 1-inch-thick (2.5 cm) rounds
- 1 lb. (454 g) pork loin or pork shoulder

Toppings

- 1 lb. (454 g) ground pork
- ½ tsp salt, plus more to season and to taste
- Black pepper, to taste
- 3 tbsp (45 ml) plus
- 1 tsp vegetable oil, divided
- 3 tbsp (30 g) garlic, minced
- 1½ tsp sugar, divided
- 2 or 3 shallots, minced
- ½ cup (75 g) Chinese salted preserved radish, minced (optional; you can buy this at an Asian food store)
- 7 oz (200 g) pork liver Splash rice vinegar
- 12 prawns, peeled with tail on and deveined

Noodle Bowl

- 21 oz (600 g) dried hủ tiếu dai noodles
- 1 bunch garlic chives (3½ oz, or 100 g), cut into 3-inch (7.5 cm) lengths or chopped 12 quail eggs, hard-boiled for 4 minutes
- Fresh greens such as lettuce, Asian celery, and chrysanthemum
- 7 oz (200 g) bean sprouts
- 3 bird's eye chili peppers, thinly sliced 1 lime, cut into wedges

Instructions:

For Broth: Tear dried squid into small chunks. Soak squid and shrimp in hot water for at least 15 minutes. Drain and rinse well.

In a stockpot, place the bones - add water – make sure bones are covered. Allow to boil, cooking for 5-10 minutes. Drain and rinse the bones.

Move bones back to a now cleaned stockpot and fill with water. Add onion, rock sugar, salt, daikon rounds, pork loin, and shrimp. Let boil and skim off the scum. Reduce heat to low. Leave the stockpot uncovered and let it simmer, for 1 to 2 hours. The pork loin may take 40 to 55 minutes to cook so take it out of the **Broth** when done – you can add it back in later. Occasionally skim off the scum. Always ensure you have the same amount of **Broth** as when you started – feel free to add more water when needed.

For toppings: Place the ground pork in a large bowl and season with the ½ tsp salt and black pepper. Add a splash of water and stir to separate the meat chunks.

Heat 3 tbsp. (45 ml) of the vegetable oil in a med pan. Add the garlic to the pan and fry until golden brown. Transfer to a bowl and mix with ½ tsp of the sugar (this keeps the garlic crispy). Repeat this step with the shallot.

Stir-fry the minced preserved radish (if using) in the same pan as the garlic and shallot with the remaining 1 tsp vegetable oil. Season lightly with salt and the remaining ½ tsp sugar.

Place the pork liver in a separate med saucepan and fill with enough water to cover it. Add the ½ tsp salt and vinegar. Bring to a boil cook until done, about 15 minutes. Let cool and thinly slice.

When you pierce the pork loin with a chopstick and see no pink water coming out, it is cooked. Remove the meat from the stockpot and rinse under cold running water. Let cool, then thinly slice into bite-size pieces.

Place the seasoned ground pork in a strainer and put into the stockpot until cooked. Use chopsticks to break up the lumps. Remove and transfer to a plate. Do the same with the fresh prawns.

To assemble the noodle bowls: Cook the noodles following the package instructions.

Fill the serving bowls with a handful of the cooked noodles. Top with ground pork, pork loin, quail eggs, pork liver, prawns, garlic chives, and fried garlic, fried shallot, and radish.

For the soup, put in soup over the noodles toppings. Serve Black Sauce (if using) alongside the dry noodle dish and a separate bowl of soup.

Serve with a platter of the fresh greens, bean sprouts, chili pepper slices, and lime wedges.

20. Pho Pizza

In Vietnam, you will find this dish (phở áp chảo) served at night at Chinese noodle stores. Besides beef, you can also use seafood (such as shrimp and squid), or if you are feeling adventurous, pig organs.

Time: 30 minutes

Makes: 2 servings

Ingredients:

- 10½ oz (300 g) beef tenderloin, thinly sliced against the grain
- Salt, to taste Black pepper, to taste
- 6 tbsp (90 ml) vegetable oil, divided
- 2 tbsp (20 g) garlic, divided, minced
- 1 tbsp (18 g) oyster sauce, divided
- 1 tbsp tapioca starch or cornstarch, divided
- 10½ oz (300 g) fresh/cooked pho noodles, separated, divided
- 1 small carrot, sliced into thin rounds
- 1 red bell pepper, into 1-inch (2.5 cm) squares
- 1 small yellow bell pepper, cut into 1-inch squares
- ½ med yellow onion, peeled and cut into wedges
- 7 oz (200 g) Chinese celery, cut into 2-inch (5 cm) lengths
- 7 oz (200 g) bok choy, leaves separated and rinsed
- ½ tsp chicken stock powder, plus more to taste
- 1 tbsp dark soy sauce, + extra to taste
- ¼ cup (60 ml) water
- 1 tablespoon (10 g) crispy fried shallot (hành phi; you can buy these at an Asian food store)
- 1 bird's eye chili pepper, thinly sliced

Instructions:

Season the beef with salt, black pepper, 1 tablespoon of the vegetable oil, 1 tablespoon (10 g) of the garlic, ½ tablespoon (9 g) of the oyster sauce, and ½ tablespoon (7.5 ml) of the tapioca starch. Mix then let it sit for about 15 minutes.

For crispy noodles, heat 3 tablespoons (45 ml) of the vegetable oil in an 8-inch (20 cm) pan over med heat. When the oil is hot, add 1/2 of the pho noodles. Use a spatula to press the noodles, so they stick together and form into a "cake." Fry both sides until golden brown. Remove from the pan place on a paper towel–lined plate to drain the excess oil. Repeat with the remaining pho noodles. Set aside.

Add one tbsp of oil in a pan over med-high heat. Add the remaining 1 tablespoon (10 g) garlic and cook and stir until fragrant. Toss in the beef and stir-fry over high heat until no longer pink on the outside. Transfer the beef back to the bowl it was marinating in.

Keeping the heat on high, add the remaining 1 tablespoon vegetable oil to the wok along with the carrot. Fry for 1 min, then add the bell peppers and onion. Stir-fry for 1 to 2 minutes, then add the Chinese celery and bok choy.

Reduce the heat to very low and season the vegetables with the ½ teaspoon chicken stock powder, 1 tablespoon dark soy sauce, and remaining ½ tablespoon (9 g) oyster sauce. Mix well.

Increase the heat to med. Combine the remaining ½ tablespoon (7.5 ml) tapioca starch with the water and add to the stir-fry. Return the beef combine well. Cook for 1-2 more mins, until the sauce turns translucent and is slightly thickened. Taste and adjust the flavor with soy sauce and/or stock powder. Turn off the heat.

Cut the crispy pho bases into triangle slices and place on a serving platter. Top with the stir-fry. Sprinkle some black pepper, fried shallot, and chili pepper slices on top. Serve hot while the noodle base is still crispy.

21. Shrimp and Noodle Pho

This noodle soup is both easy to make and delicious at the same time!

Time: 30 minutes

Makes: 2

Ingredients:

- 9 cups water
- 3 ramen noodle packets
- 10 oz. frozen, cooked, peeled and deveined med shrimp
- 2 tsp dark oriental sesame oil
- ½ tsp crushed red pepper.
- 1 cup scallions, chopped
- ½ cup carrots, grated

Instructions:

Take a clean and dry pot and add the water to it. Bring this up to a boil. Now break the blocks of noodles into 4 pieces each and add them to the pot. Cook for around 5 minutes while constantly stirring. This will ensure that the strands separate from each other. Cook until the noodles are tender.

Take the pot off the heat now. Add the shrimp and the packets of seasoning to the pot immediately. Also add the oil and the crushed peppers.

Let cool for around 2 minutes. Sprinkle the scallions and carrots over the top. You may grate some cheese over the top if you want to. Serve hot with lime wedges.

22. Roast pork noodle soup

Meaty, fragrant and full of absolute deliciousness!

Time: 30m

Serves: 4

Ingredients:

- 7 oz dried pho noodles
- ½ bunch gai laan (Chinese broccoli) about 11 oz
- 3 tbsp peanut oil
- 6 slices of ginger, cut into matchsticks
- 1 tbsp Shaoxing wine, or dry sherry
- 2 tbsp oyster sauce
- 2 tbsp soy sauce
- ½ tsp salt
- pinch of black pepper
- 2 tsp sugar
- ½ tsp sesame oil
- 1 tbsp cornstarch, mixed with little water
- 7 oz char sieu (red roast pork), cut into thin slices
- 2 spring onions, sliced diagonally into 1 inch lengths
- cups chicken stock
- 1 spring onion, green part only, sliced into 1 inch lengths

Instructions:

Cook firstly noodles in plenty of salted, boiling water for 4 minutes, or until tender, then rinse well under cold water. Drain and set aside.

Cut gai laan into 2½ pieces. Put thick stems in a pot of boiling water and cook for 1 minute. Add leaves and thinner stems and cook for 20 seconds. Remove from pot and plunge into cold water. When cool, drain and set aside.

Heat peanut oil and stir fry ginger for 60 seconds, add gai laan and stir fry for another minute. Add rice wine, oyster sauce, soy sauce, salt, pepper, sugar, sesame oil and cornstarch mixture. When liquid starts to boil, add pork and spring onion and heat through, stirring.

In your separate pot, bring chicken stock to the boil. Put noodles in a strainer or colander and pour boiling water over the top to warm them. Drain well. To serve, put a handful of noodles into each of 4 bowls. Pour chicken stock over noodles and top with pork mixture. Scatter spring onion on top and serve with spoons and chopsticks.

23. Thai Shrimp Noodle Soup

This delicious Thai noodle soup is super delicious and easy to make! The best part? It's pretty healthy too!

Time: 35 minutes

Makes: 2

Ingredients:

- 10 oz. med-size shrimp, peeled and deveined
- 2 ½ tbsp. fish sauce or soy sauce
- 3 carrots, thinly sliced
- 2 garlic cloves, finely minced
- 2 tsp fresh basil, chopped
- 3 cups fresh spinach, coarsely chopped
- 10 cups water
- 3 packets of chicken flavored Ramen noodles
- 4 green onions, minced
- 2 tbsp. Thai hot chili sauce
- 1 cup mushrooms, sliced
- Juice and grated zest from 1 ½ limes

Instructions:

Fill a large pot with water. Bring this water to a boil on a high flame. Add the carrots, fish sauce, green onions, ginger, garlic, basil and chili sauce.

Break the noodles and put them into the water as well. Keep stirring to separate the strands. Now add the seasoning from 2 packets that came with the noodles. Boil for 5 minutes or so. After this, add the shrimp, mushrooms and spinach. Cook for another 5 minutes. Top with lime zest and juice, and stir well.

24. Penang laksa

When most people think of laksa, they think of curry laksa, or laksa lemak. But the people of Penang have devised their own laksa using fish. Rather than thick, creamy and coconutty, this laksa is sour and **Broth**y – a totally different kettle of fish.

Time: 20 minutes

Makes: 4

Ingredients:

- 4 cups cold water
- ½ tsp salt
- 1 lb. blue mackerel, or other firm-fleshed fish
- 2 cups tamarind water
- 2 stalks of lemongrass, white part only, finely sliced
- 2 tsp ground turmeric
- 1 tbsp belacan (shrimp paste)
- 6 dried chilies, soaked, drained and chopped
- ¾ inch piece galangal or ginger, finely chopped
- 1 tbsp palm sugar, or white sugar
- 10 oz round rice noodles or Hokkien noodles
- 1 cucumber, peeled and cut into the thin matchsticks

Instructions:

Bring water and salt to the boil, add fish and simmer for 5 minutes. Remove fish, cool, then flake off flesh with your hands and set aside. Return heads and bones to the water. Add tamarind water and simmer for a further 10 minutes, then strain through a fine sieve and set stock aside.

Pound or blend lemongrass, turmeric, belacan, chilies and galangal to a paste. Add to fish stock with sugar and simmer for 10 minutes. Add fish and heat through.

Pour boiling water over noodles in a heatproof bowl. Drain and divide noodles among 4 warm serving bowls. Add soup and top with cucumber.

25. Egg flower noodle soup

This is a serious version of good old chicken and sweet corn soup, but without the chicken and the sweet corn.

Time: 1 hour

Makes: 4

Ingredients:

- 10 oz. pork belly
- ¼ cup dried wood fungus
- 8 dried shiitake mushrooms
- 2 tbsp peanut oil
- 1 tbsp fresh ginger, minced
- 3 spring onions, green part only, finely sliced
- ½ cup bamboo shoots, cut into matchsticks
- 4 cups chicken stock
- 1 tsp salt
- 2 tbsp soy sauce
- 1 tbsp Shaoxing wine or dry sherry
- 11 oz. fresh flat egg noodles
- ½ cup ham, sliced into thin strips
- 1 tbsp cornstarch, mixed with little water
- 2 eggs, beaten
- 1 tsp sesame oil
- ½ tsp pepper

Instructions:

Put pork belly in a saucepan, cover with cold water and bring to the boil. Skim off any nasty stuff, reduce heat and simmer for 45 minutes. Turn off the heat and leave pork in the liquid to cool.

Soak the wood fungus and mushrooms separately in hot water for about an hour. Drain and rinse well, then cut into thin strips, discarding any stems.

Cut the cooled pork into thin strips about 1" wide (reserve the cooking liquid, skimming off the fat).

Next, heat peanut oil in a saucepan and cook ginger, mushrooms, wood fungus and bamboo shoots and stir fry briefly. Add chicken stock and 4 cups of the pork cooking liquid and bring to the boil. Add salt, soy sauce and rice wine, taste, adjust seasonings, and simmer for 3 minutes.

Cook noodles in boiling water for about 1 minute, then drain, rinse in cold water and drain again. Return to the saucepan, off the heat, and keep warm.

Add pork and ham to the soup, turn up the heat and stir in the cornstarch mixture. Stir until the soup thickens, lower heat and slowly pour the egg into the soup in a thin stream through the tines of a fork. Stir lightly, then add sesame oil and pepper. Divide noodles between 4 bowls. Ladle soup over and scatter with spring onions.

BONUS: Appetizers

Below, you'll find some delicious Vietnamese appetizers that go perfectly with your Pho dishes!

26. Spring rolls

Refreshing, light, and full of flavor, fresh spring rolls (gỏi cuốn) are one of Vietnam's world-famous dishes. The dipping sauce is what makes all the difference; the richness of the peanut butter complements the sweet tanginess of the hoisin sauce.

Time: 45 minutes

Makes: 15 rolls

Ingredients

Spring rolls

- 10½ oz (300 g) pork belly
- 1 tsp salt
- 7 oz (200 g) shrimp (about 15 total)
- 7 oz (200 g) rice vermicelli noodles
- Fresh greens and herbs such as lettuce, mint, cilantro, and perilla,
- 1 cucumber, cut into 3 x 1-inch (7 x 2.5 cm) lengths
- 15 rice paper wrappers (8½ inch, or 22 cm, in diameter)
- 5 garlic chives, cut into 4-inch (20 cm) lengths (optional)

Dipping sauce

- 1 tbsp vegetable oil
- 1 tbsp (10 g) garlic, minced
- 5 tbsp (80 g) hoisin sauce
- 1 tbsp (16 g) peanut butter
- 1 tbsp sugar
- 1 tsp minced bird's eye chili pepper
- 1 tbsp (9 g) roasted peanuts, crushed

Instructions:

For rolls: fill a med saucepan half-full of water and bring to a rolling boil. Add the pork belly and salt.

Bring to a boil again and reduce the heat to med and cook for 25 - 35 minutes, depending on the thickness of your pork cut. To test the pork, pierce the meat with a chopstick or fork and when the water coming out runs clear, not pink, it's cooked through. Remove the pork and soak in cold water for 5 minutes to prevent it from darkening. Drain and let cool. Reserve the **Broth** for later use.

In a large pan, cook the shrimp, without oil, over med heat for 1 to 2 minutes, until they turn orange. Let cool and peel. Slice each shrimp in half lengthwise. Remove any black lines running through the shrimp meat.

Cook the rice vermicelli noodles in boiling water for 3 - 5 minutes, until soft (or follow package instructions). Drain. Rinse then the noodles with cold water to stop the cooking.

For the sauce: heat vegetable oil in a small pan over med-high heat. Add the garlic and fry until golden brown. Add the hoisin sauce, 5 tbsp. (75 ml) of the reserved pork **Broth**, peanut butter, and sugar to the pan. Stir well and simmer over low heat for 1 to 2 minutes, until slightly thickened. Pour the sauce into condiment bowls and top with the minced chili peppers and crushed peanuts.

To assemble the rolls: place the cooked noodles, shrimp, pork, fresh greens, and sliced cucumber on plates. Prepare a pan of lukewarm water to soften the rice paper and find a flat work surface (like a cutting board or large plate) for the rolling job.

Dip one piece of rice paper into the water, covering the paper with water without soaking it. Gently shake off the excess water. Lay it on the flat surface.

Place the fresh vegetables in a row, from left to right, on the lower third of the rice paper wrappers, leaving about 2 inches (5 cm) on both sides. Next, place some noodles, cucumber slices, 2 pork slices, and 2 shrimp halves on the rice paper, in rows parallel to the vegetables. Keep the orange sides of the shrimp facing down.

Starting from the end closest to the filling, roll once or twice until you reach the center of the rice paper. Fold then the left and right sides inward and continue rolling. You can also add a garlic chive at the end to give the roll a little "tail." Repeat these steps for the remaining 14 rolls.

To serve, either spoon some dipping sauce onto the rolls or dip them into the sauce. You can also cut the rolls on the diagonal in half Form more manageable to eat. Serve the rolls within 2 hours of wrapping. (if you are going on the picnic, you can wrap the rolls in plastic to keep them fresh for a few hours longer. It will prevent the rice paper from drying out and becoming sticky.)

27. San choy bau with cellophane noodles

With its minced meat, water chestnuts, mushrooms and bamboo shoots inside a crisp, fresh lettuce leaf, san choy bau manages to roll up all the principles of Chinese cooking in one neat little parcel.

Time: 15 minutes

Makes: 8

Ingredients:

- 2 oz bean thread vermicelli
- 2 fresh quails
- 6 dried shiitake mushrooms, soaked
- 3 tbsp peanut oil
- 2 slices ginger, finely chopped
- 7 oz bamboo shoots, finely chopped
- 1 clove of garlic, finely chopped
- 6 water chestnuts, finely chopped
- 5 oz minced pork or chicken
- 1 slice leg ham, diced
- 1 tsp sugar
- ½ tsp salt
- pinch of white pepper
- 1 tbsp dark soy sauce
- 1 tbsp hoisin sauce
- 1 tbsp dry sherry
- 2 tbsp chicken stock
- 1:1 mixture of cornstarch and water (1 tsp each)
- ½ tsp sesame oil
- 8 perfect lettuce leaves, washed and dried

Instructions:

Put noodles in a heatproof bowl and pour boiling water over to cover. Leave for 3 to 4 minutes. Drain and rinse under cold water. With a pair of scissors, cut into roughly 2 inch lengths.

Remove meat from quails, chop finely and set aside. Drain mushrooms, stem, and finely slice caps. Heat oil and stir fry mushrooms and ginger for 1 minute. Add bamboo shoots, garlic and water chestnuts and stir fry for 30 seconds. Add quail meat, pork or chicken, ham, sugar, salt and pepper and stir fry over high heat for 3 minutes. Add noodles, soy sauce, hoisin sauce, rice wine, chicken stock and cornstarch mixture and cook for another 60 seconds or until it starts to thicken. Sprinkle sesame oil on top, spoon into lettuce cups and serve. To eat, roll up the cup and eat with your fingers.

28. Cubed Radish Kimchi

This is the classic hot and fermented pickle that is brilliant on rice or stir-fried with beef or tofu.

Time: 1 – 3 days

Makes: 3 cups

Ingredients:

- 2 pounds daikon radish
- 1 tbsp plus 2 tsp fine sea salt
- 2 tbsp sugar
- 2 large garlic cloves, minced
- 1 (¾-inch) piece unpeeled fresh ginger, minced
- ¼ cup Korean chili flakes
- 2 tbsp fish sauce

Instructions:

Peel firstly the radish and chop into bite-sized cubes. In a large bowl, toss the radish cubes with the salt and sugar. Rest 30 minutes, stirring once halfway through.

Next, drain the radish, discarding the liquid. Return the radish to the bowl. Toss it with the garlic, chili flakes, ginger, and fish sauce, and pack it down firmly into the bowl.

Place then a layer of plastic wrap over the radish, allowing space for air to come in through the edges. Move to a cool, dark place for 1 - 3 days, stirring once each day, until it has a pleasingly fermented aroma.

To store, pack into a shallow square or rectangular container, ideally glass or ceramic, which won't retain odors. This pickle will keep in the refrigerator for at least 2 weeks.

29. Mushrooms in Soy Sauce (Pyogo Bohsot)

This makes the dish feel more like a pickle and less like a side dish. If crimini mushrooms aren't luxurious enough for you, feel free to substitute shiitakes in their place.

Time: 1½ hours

Makes: about 2 cups

Ingredients:

- 6 tbsp Japanese soy sauce
- 1 tsp Korean chile flakes
- 2 tbsp. plus 1 tsp light brown sugar
- 3 tbsp unseasoned rice vinegar
- 1 (⅓-inch) piece ginger, peeled and minced very fine
- 1 small garlic clove, minced
- Green tops from 2 green onions, sliced into thin rings
- 1 pound crimini mushrooms

Instructions:

Put a large pot of water on to boil. In the meantime, prep the marinade. Combine the soy sauce, chile flakes, sugar, vinegar, ginger, garlic, and green onion. Set aside.

Wash and drain the mushrooms. Trim and discard the tough tips of their stems and slice them lengthwise ¼ inch thick. Cook the sliced mushrooms in the boiling water for 30 seconds, stirring continuously. Use a large slotted spoon to remove the mushrooms from the pot into a colander; reserve the water for later use as soup stock or to boil pasta. Or if you'd rather not fuss with that, simply drain the mushrooms through a colander. Rinse mushrooms under cold water to stop the cooking, stirring with your hands. Drain the mushrooms very well and use a clean kitchen towel or paper towels to blot off excess water.

Add the mushrooms to the marinade and stir thoroughly to combine. Allow the mushrooms to sit at room temperature for 1 hour before eating. Can be covered and in the refrigerator for at least a month.

30. Wontons

This recipe makes crispy, crunchy and delicious beef wontons!

Time: 40 minutes

Makes: 2

Ingredients

- 8 wonton wrappers
- Sea salt and pepper
- 1/2 lb. ground lamb
- 1 C. Greek yogurt, placed in a cheesecloth-lined sieve and nicely drained overnight in the fridge
- 1 tsp garlic, minced
- 1/3 C. onion, minced
- 4 tsp dried mint
- 2 tbsp. fresh parsley, minced
- 1 jalapeño pepper, minced

Instructions:

In a bowl, add the lamb, onion, salt, parsley, garlic, jalapeño pepper and black pepper and mix well. Refrigerate to chill completely.

Arrange the wrapper onto a smooth surface. Place a tsp of the lamb mixture over each wrapper and fold to form a half circle, sealing with wet fingers. Arrange the dumplings onto baking sheet dusted with the cornstarch.

In a pan of the rapidly boiling salted water, add the dumplings and stir once. Cook for about 2 minutes. Transfer onto a paper towels lined plate to drain. In a large sauté pan, add yogurt on med heat and cook till warmed. Add the hot dumplings and toss to coat well. Divide the dumpling mixture into serving bowls and serve with a sprinkling of the dried mint.

Conclusion

Well, there you go! 30 delicious Pho recipes for you to try at home. Make sure you try out all the recipes in this book and don't forget to share these pho delicacies with your friends and family!

About the Author

A native of Indianapolis, Indiana, Valeria Ray found her passion for cooking while she was studying English Literature at Oakland City University. She decided to try a cooking course with her friends and the experience changed her forever. She enrolled at the Art Institute of Indiana which offered extensive courses in the culinary Arts. Once Ray dipped her toe in the cooking world, she never looked back.

When Valeria graduated, she worked in French restaurants in the Indianapolis area until she became the head chef at one of the 5-star establishments in the area. Valeria's attention to taste and visual detail caught the eye of a local business person who expressed an interest in publishing her recipes. Valeria began her secondary career authoring cookbooks and e-books which she tackled with as much talent and gusto as her first career. Her passion for food leaps off the page of her books which have colourful anecdotes and stunning pictures of dishes she has prepared herself.

Valeria Ray lives in Indianapolis with her husband of 15 years, Tom, her daughter, Isobel and their loveable Golden Retriever, Goldy. Valeria enjoys cooking special dishes in her large, comfortable kitchen where the family gets involved in preparing meals. This successful, dynamic chef is an inspiration to culinary students and novice cooks everywhere.

Author's Afterthoughts

Thank you for Purchasing my book and taking the time to read it from front to back. I am always grateful when a reader chooses my work and I hope you enjoyed it!

With the vast selection available online, I am touched that you chose to be purchasing my work and take valuable time out of your life to read it. My hope is that you feel you made the right decision.

I very much would like to know what you thought of the book. Please take the time to write an honest and informative review on Amazon.com. Your experience and opinions will be of great benefit to me and those readers looking to make an informed choice.

With much thanks,

Valeria Ray